On the Emergence of an Ecological Class – a Memo

On the Emergence of an Ecological Class – a Memo

Subject: How to promote the emergence of an ecological class that's self-aware and proud

By: **Bruno Latour and Nikolaj Schultz**

Date: January 2022

To: Members of ecological parties and their present and future electors

Translated by: Julie Rose

polity

Originally published in French as *Mémo sur la nouvelle classe écologique. Comment faire émerger une classe écologique consciente et fière d'elle-même.* © Editions La Découverte, Paris, 2022

This English edition © Polity Press, 2022

Polity Press
65 Bridge Street
Cambridge CB2 1UR, UK

Polity Press
111 River Street
Hoboken, NJ 07030, USA

ISBN-13: 978-1-5095-5505-5 – hardback
ISBN-13: 978-1-5095-5506-2 – paperback

A catalogue record for this book is available from the British Library.

Library of Congress Control Number: 2022939600

Typeset in 10.5 on 15.5pt Plantin MT Pro
by Cheshire Typesetting Ltd, Cuddington, Cheshire
Printed and bound in the UK by CPI Group (UK) Ltd, Croydon

The publisher has used its best endeavours to ensure that the URLs for external websites referred to in this book are correct and active at the time of going to press. However, the publisher has no responsibility for the websites and can make no guarantee that a site will remain live or that the content is or will remain appropriate.

Every effort has been made to trace all copyright holders, but if any have been overlooked the publisher will be pleased to include any necessary credits in any subsequent reprint or edition.

For further information on Polity, visit our website: politybooks.com

The Authors

Bruno Latour has been working for over fifteen years on issues of political philosophy relating to what he calls the New Climate Regime. Nikolaj Schultz is finishing a thesis in sociology at the University of Copenhagen on what he terms the geosocial classes. Neither has any official position in any of the existing ecological movements, but both are aware of the need to provide political expressions of ecology with a broader base than the one mobilised till now. This is what authorises these two authors to draw up here a provisional list of points that it's important we reflect on together to amplify the multipronged action of activists and numerous political leaders. It's written in the style of a memo, so you won't find nuances or notes.

Memorandum

A. A note you jot down to make it easier to remember something; through metonymy, a notebook or exercise book in which you note what you want to recall.

B. A note on an important topic written by an embassy or consular diplomat setting out, for the government they're posted to, the point of view of their own government on a given issue.

Contents

I

Class struggles and classification struggles

1. Under what conditions can ecology organise politics around itself instead of just being one group of movements among others? Can it aspire to define the political horizon as did, at other times, liberalism followed by the various socialisms, then neoliberalism and finally, more recently, the illiberal or neofascist parties, whose influence seemingly never ceases to grow? Can it learn from social history how new political movements emerge and how they win the battle of ideas, well before being able to translate the advances they make into parties and elections?

2. Ecology urgently needs to acquire more coherence and more autonomy, given the collapse of the 'international order', the enormity of the catastrophe under way, and the general dissatisfaction with the political platform of the traditional parties as revealed by high levels of voter abstention. Now, if there are plenty of ecological movements out there and even parties that adopt ecology as their banner, these are nonetheless far from being movements or parties that define, in their own way and *on their own terms*, the battlefronts around them that would allow them to pinpoint the whole raft of allies and adversaries in the political landscape. Several decades after starting out, they remain dependent on the old divides, and this limits their search for alliances and diminishes the leeway they have. If it really wants to have any clout, political ecology must not let itself be defined by others, and must identify, by itself and for itself, the new sources of injustice it has spotted and the new battlefronts it has discovered.

3. Because it relied on concern for the nature that was known to Science and external to the social world, political ecology too long hinged on a *pedagogical* version of its action: once the catastrophic situation was known, action would necessarily follow. But it's become clear that, far from putting an end to or diverting attention away from social conflicts, the call for 'the protection of nature' has, on the contrary, multiplied those conflicts. From the Gilets jaunes in France to the demonstrations of young people all over the place, via the protests of farmers in India, indigenous communities resisting fracking in North America, or the disputes over the impact of electric vehicles, the message is clear: conflicts are only proliferating. Talking about nature doesn't mean signing a peace treaty; it means recognising the existence of a whole host of conflicts on all possible subjects involving everyday existence, at all scales and over all continents. Nature doesn't unify – it divides.

4. Curiously, ecological concerns – in any case, those regarding climate, energy and biodiversity – have become ubiquitous. But the host of conflicts has not, for the moment anyway, taken the form of a general mobilisation the way the transformations triggered by liberalism and socialism were able to do in the past few centuries. Ecology, in this sense, is both everywhere and nowhere. For the moment, it seems that the immense diversity of conflicts is preventing these struggles from being given a coherent definition. Well, this diversity isn't a flaw, it's an asset. That's because ecology is engaged in a general exploration of living conditions that have been destroyed by the obsession with production alone. For the ecological movement to gain in coherence and autonomy, and for this to be translated into a historic momentum comparable to what was seen in the past, its project needs to be recognised, embraced, understood and represented effectively by gathering all these conflicts into a single unity of action comprehensible to all. To do this, we first need to accept that ecology implies division; then to offer a convincing cartography of the new types of conflict it generates; and, lastly, to define a common horizon for collective action.

5. If it's true that ecology is both everywhere and nowhere at once, it's also true that, on the one hand, a conflict situation is opening up on all subjects, and, on the other, a sort of indifference, of irenicism, of expectation and bogus peace prevails. Each new publication put out by the IPCC produces impassioned reactions, but, as in operas, the marching songs, 'March on, march on, before it's too late!', don't shift the choruses on stage more than a few metres. 'Everything has to change radically', yet nothing changes. So, if it's crucial that we recognise a generalised state of war, we still have to admit that, for the minute, it's hard to draw up clear fronts between friends and enemies. On countless subjects, we are ourselves divided, both victims and accomplices at the same time. Whereas in the preceding century, they could draw up, if roughly, the class conflicts that allowed people to, say, vote for parties with recognisable ideologies, it's hard to do that today as long as the state of ecological war has not been clarified. How can we talk about class conflict if the ecological class itself isn't clearly defined?

6. It's always a bit anxiety-making to reuse the notion of 'class'. That's why we need to resist the temptation to invoke the notion of 'class struggle' just like that, even while recognising that this notion was able to serve a major purpose, last century, by simplifying and unifying the various forms of mobilisation. Its advantage as a concept was to allow a delineation of the structure of the social and material world, by moving the political dynamics on in terms of social conflicts and of developing experiences and collective horizons. Its role over the course of history was clearly *descriptive* every bit as much as *performative*: it claimed to describe social reality, allowing people to position themselves in the landscape they inhabited, but it was never separated from some project or other of transforming society. So, to talk about 'class' always means getting ready for battle. Similarly, to talk about enabling the emergence of an 'ecological class' is necessarily to offer both a new *description* and new *perspectives* for action at the same time. The classification operation, for this class taking shape that we're calling 'ecological', is necessarily performative. Hence the usefulness of reusing the term 'class', even if it brings a lot of confusion with it.

7. If it's hard to reuse the notion of 'class struggle', that's because the issue of ecology has turned it into a *classification struggle*. No one agrees on what makes up the class they're part of. People who belong to the same class (in the classical social or cultural sense) feel completely alien to their peers as soon as ecological conflicts crop up. Others, conversely, recognise as their 'brothers in arms' activists who, from a social or cultural standpoint, belong to quite different life forms. When it comes to ecology, we encounter some pretty strange bedfellows. Hence the effect of disorientation which explains a large part of the present brutalisation of public life: on ecological subjects, allies are no more aligned than adversaries. It's enough to drive anyone mad. So, to promote the emergence of an ecological class, we have to accept this *struggle over classifications* and find distinguishing criteria that either cut across, or occasionally, on the contrary, fit in with, traditional class conflicts. Despite the shadow cast by the tradition of 'class struggle', political ecology can't avoid this uncertainty about class affiliations. It must keep on asking the question: 'When disputes involve ecology, who do you feel close to and who do you feel terribly far away from?' The emergence of a potential 'class consciousness' comes at this cost.

II

A prodigious extension of materialism

8. If it wants to become autonomous, ecology has to agree to give the term 'class' a new meaning. Well, for the moment, the ecological class is still afraid of not knowing how to position itself in its relationship to the struggles of the past two centuries. For instance, it's easily intimidated by the accusation that it's not 'left-wing' enough. As long as this point isn't cleared up, it will never be able to define its battles by and for itself. And yet, there is indeed a historic continuity with the struggles of societies to resist the economisation of all ties. Because it contests the notion of production, we might even say that the ecological class substantially amplifies the general refusal to grant the economy autonomy *at the expense of* societies. In this sense, no doubt about it, it is certainly on the left, and even *fairly and squarely*.

9. And yet, the situation just isn't the same when it comes to aligning with the tradition of 'class struggle', the expression of which remains profoundly bound up with the idea and ideal of production. Even if it's always tempting to get a new situation to fit into a recognised framework, it would be prudent not to rush to assert that the ecological class is simply extending 'anti-capitalist' struggles. Ecology is right not to let its values be dictated to it by what has become, largely, a sort of conditioned reflex. So, it's important to evacuate this quarrel and to understand why, on this score, there isn't necessarily any continuity. That's the grain of truth in the cliché 'neither right nor left'. And it has nothing to do with some alleged 'transcending' of socialist ideals.

10. A number of analysts successively reworked the notion of class as the social fabric changed shape over the course of the twentieth century, but Marx remains an indispensable guide for venturing onto this terrain. For a very precise period in history, 'class theory' offered a compass that gave people a clear sense of what allowed them to subsist, of where they were situated in the social landscape, and of who they were fighting against. In the modern sense of the terms, 'class', 'class interests' and 'class struggles', not to mention the highly contested 'class consciousness', have been used to describe how different individuals shared, or didn't share, their conditions of subsistence with others; how social groups occupied different positions in a stratified material and social landscape; and lastly, how antagonistic relationships between the interests of those groups inevitably made them clash in social and political conflicts. This is why the influence of the various brands of socialism on sociology and political culture was so great. Like liberalism, Marxism made sense of history. If the ecological class wants to make a real impact, it too has to do *at least as well* and define the direction of history. . . only, of *its* history!

11. What the Marxist definition of class offered us was an understanding of *material* conditions, of which social conditions are merely an expression. Marx's compass was useful because it relied on a relatively clear description of the processes necessary to the continuation of society. It begins with a *description* of the mechanisms by means of which societies are reproduced; then it *classifies* the way the actors are positioned in antagonistic fashion within that reproduction process. In this sense, an analysis in terms of class can be said to be *materialist*. So, if the ecological class wants to follow this tradition as its logical inheritance, it has to accept the lesson of the Marxist tradition and define itself – *it, too* – in relation to the *material conditions* of its existence. The new class struggle must rely on an approach that's every bit as materialist as the old one. This is the essential point where there's evident continuity.

12. But here's the thing: *it's no longer the same materiality!* That's the reason for the relative discontinuity between the socialist traditions and the entity whose emergence needs to be fostered today. Just as there's a conflict over classifications, there's a conflict over what constitutes a materialist analysis of living conditions. For Marx, human survival and reproduction

11

were the first principle of all societies and their history. And so, the initial step in any analysis of human society or social history was necessarily to account for the material conditions – what humans ate, the water they drank, the clothes they wore, the houses they lived in, etc. – that allow human societies and collectives to subsist, as well as the processes that gave birth to them. It's the production of these material conditions of reproduction that Marx saw as the foundation of social history. But above all it was a matter of the reproduction *of humans*. Well, today we find ourselves in a quite different historical configuration. We're not in the same history any more. Production no longer defines our sole horizon. And, more than anything else, we're no longer faced with the same *material reality*.

13. What happens when the very definition of material existence is in the process of changing? By thinking almost exclusively in terms of *production* and *reproduction*, the socialist compass can't account for the way the class landscape is changing shape today. In parallel with the situation at the dawn of mechanical civilisation, the New Climate Regime is now forcing us to *redescribe* the processes by means of which societies reproduce themselves and continue to exist. Once again: 'All that is solid melts into air'. Just as in the nineteenth century, we are currently witnessing a huge transformation in the material infrastructure of societies. Which forces us to stop relying exclusively on the old descriptions to answer the question of how collectives continue to subsist, how their means of subsistence can be maintained over the long haul, and how their history needs to be written. Analysis in terms of an ecological class remains materialist, but it needs to turn to phenomena other than the production and reproduction of human beings alone.

14. Just after the Second World War, those systems of production accelerated so fast they destabilised the Earth systems and climate systems – something the terms 'Anthropocene' and 'Great Acceleration' sum up pretty well. We are now witnessing the way climate mutations are dramatically intensifying and transforming the forces that ensure the continuity and survival of societies. The system of production has become a synonym for *system of destruction*. What would a Marxist analysis that also focuses on the reproduction of non-humans entail? Being materialist, today, means that, on top of the reproduction of material conditions favourable to human beings, we need to take into account the habitability conditions of planet Earth. These conditions force us to consider not only what the *political economy* of the traditional parties sought to simplify under the label *resource*, but a new material reality of the planet. The economy directed its attention to the mobilisation of resources with an eye to *production*, but does there exist an economy capable of *turning back* to maintaining the habitability conditions of the terrestrial world? In other words, of *turning its back* on paying attention exclusively to production so as to embed it back into the quest for conditions of habitability? That, in a nutshell, is the whole point of the new ecological class. On this score, understandably, the discontinuity with the traditional 'class struggle' is pretty clear.

15. This discordance over the materialist analysis of class in the end allows us to see how far analysis in terms of ecological class *extends* and *renews* the traditional struggles of the left – but in its own way. It's definitely a matter of turning away from the exclusive focus on production in such a way as to amplify the *resistance of society* (to take up Karl Polanyi's expression) to economisation. Some of the struggles of the twentieth century were obviously inspired by the Marxist tradition, but plenty of others were fought simply in the name of a rejection of the expansion of production and against the insufferable claim that has always been made that production is somehow not embedded in the rest of social life. As Lucas Chancel puts it: 'The abolition of slavery, social security, universal suffrage, free education, are not strictly speaking issues to do with the organisation of material production.' These were vital expressions of the impossibility for a human society to let itself be defined by economisation alone. Criticising certain limits of Marxist-inspired materialism, then, also allows us to revive the multiple traditions of struggle against economisation. So, except for this slight difference, decisive it's true, the ecological class can claim to be taking up again, by amplifying it, the history of the liberating left. A sign that this take-up has indeed occurred is that there are now many more ecological activists being assassinated than unionists.

III

The great turnaround

16. To sum up the situation, we could say that by now everyone knows decisive action is needed to avert catastrophe but that the relays, motivation and direction that would allow us to act are lacking. People go on ad nauseam about 'revolution', 'radical change', 'collapse', but it's blindingly obvious that nothing has come along to translate these anxieties into a mobilising programme of action on a par with what's at stake. In this sense, the new call to action in no way resembles what our predecessors went through in wartime or during episodes of reconstruction, development or globalisation. People's energies used to flow from their ideals; understanding a situation was enough to mobilise. Today, the certainty of catastrophe seems, rather, to *paralyse* action. In any case, there's no instinctive alignment between representations of the world, energies to be harnessed, and values to be defended. Everyone's instincts, on the contrary, are turned towards a 'recovery' identical to the old way of conceiving of production. The duty of the ecological class is to diagnose the sources of this paralysis and to seek a new alignment between anxieties, collective action, ideals and the sense of history.

17. We begin to understand the sources of this paralysis when we realise that the very *direction* of action has been reversed. To simplify, we could say that, for two centuries, people's energies were easily mobilised when it was all about increasing production and making the distribution of the wealth thereby obtained *a bit less unfair*. Of course, there have been innumerable conflicts between the various forms of liberalism and the multiple socialist traditions, but those conflicts could count on a background of *complete agreement* about stepping up production. Disagreements were more about the fair distribution of its fruit. Development went indisputably with an idea of history, and people could always count on the energies unleashed by the watchword: 'Forward!' Well, today, seen from the old model, the watchword seems more like: 'Right back in time!' Suddenly, stepping up production, the very notion of development and that of progress look like so many aberrations that need to be remedied. Associating production with *destruction* of the habitability conditions of the planet entails a crisis in our mobilisation capabilities. It's not surprising, then, that the enormity of the threats predicted by the experts has so little practical effect. The fact is our mental, moral, organisational, administrative and legal equipment, so long associated with development, is running on empty because it was created to direct attention to what has become a dead end. Today, the direction of affairs has visibly changed, but the new equipment that would allow us to take action has not yet been designed. We remain stalled at anxiety, guilt and impotence. The role of the ecological class is to furnish us with that equipment.

18. The decisive change of tack is giving priority to maintaining the habitability conditions of the planet and not to developing production. In this sense, it's not just a matter of limiting 'productivism', but, as Dusan Kazik demands, of turning away completely from the horizon of production as a principle of analysis of relations between humans, and between humans and all they're learning to depend on. In actual fact, the problem with paying attention exclusively to production was that everything necessary to its march was reduced to the simple role of resources. Well, the planet engendered by living things over the course of millennia surrounds, envelops, allows, authorises, provides a great deal more than resources for human action. As the long history of the Earth shows, it's living things that have enabled the continuity of terrestrial life, which they have themselves created with the passing of billions of years – climate, atmosphere, soil and ocean included. The system of production is just one part, and not the most important one, of this whole. From being central, it has become limited; the periphery, on the other hand, has now taken up all the room. The system of production actually finds itself embedded, enveloped in an altogether different organisation, directing our attention to practices that favour the *engendering* necessary to maintaining living conditions – or that destroy them. To produce means to assemble and combine resources; it does not mean to engender, that is, to carefully induce the continuity of beings that the world's habitability depends on. Instead of the strange metaphor of development, it would be more helpful, if we want to capture this reversal, to talk about *envelopment*: all the issues of production are surrounded, wrapped up in the practices of engendering they depend on. We're used to seeing 'growth' as the sole means of getting out of trouble, forgetting about the destruction it causes, whereas *prosperity* has always depended on engendering practices. It's not a matter of 'degrowing', but of finally prospering. And yet, no conditioned reflex, no instinct, no affect as yet translates such a shift to the point where it becomes the new common sense.

19. Class conflicts, in organising the history of the past two centuries exclusively around production and the allocation of its fruits, have been wilfully and systematically blind to the *limits* of the material conditions of the planet. As a result, the ecological class can no longer define itself solely through analysis of the *mode of production*. The wedge issue that sets the new ecological class against all the others is that it wants to *restrict* the place taken up by the forces of production, while the rest of them want to *expand* it. The charming euphemism 'transition' underscores as ineptly as possible what is well and truly a violent upending. It's in relation to this tension that the new class struggle positions itself. The key issue is not, as it was before, solely about class conflicts *within* the system of production, but about the *necessarily polemical* relationship between the system of production and maintaining habitability conditions. It's this *second-tier* tension that makes for the whole novelty of the situation. The canonical classes, the ones of Marx and the liberals – the classes dependent on an economised reading of history – submit issues of habitability to the relations of production, whereas the emerging class *does the opposite*. Beneath the evidence of the modern order, it reveals genuine rifts. Beneath the class struggle, another class struggle.

20. Fighting like this to define itself as being at odds with production, the ecological class thus adds to the relations of production engendering practices that have always defined the *exterior* of human activity because they have always *surrounded* and *encompassed* the relations of production by making them possible. According to Pierre Charbonnier's definition, the ecological class defines itself through the junction, within the same enclosure, of the world *we live in* and the world *we live off*. So what it adds to production is the return of habitability conditions in which the determination to produce has always been embedded. Even though the definition of the *social* classes has always depended, in reality, on the key question of reproduction (as we see even in Marx), the burden of economisation has driven the Marxist traditions, every bit as much as the liberal traditions, to deny or minimise its importance – at least when defining classes. The class struggle has always been, but is again today becoming, explicitly, an interlocking set of *geosocial* conflicts, for which formatting through economisation is no longer appropriate, since it isn't able to make room for *terrestrials* – humans included.

IV

A class that's legitimate again

21. The ecological class, then, is the one that takes on the issue of habitability. Because of this, it has a broader, longer, more complex vision of history and even of geohistory. What at first looked like a retreat, a backward movement, almost a 'reactionary' position, now becomes an immense *expansion* of sensitivity to the conditions necessary for life. This is why the ecological class has entered into conflict with the old classes, which were incapable of grasping the underlying conditions of their projects. Neither the liberals nor the socialists seriously took their conditions of habitability into account – the neofascists even less so. In this sense, the ecological class, because it sees further, because it takes a greater number of values into account, because it's ready to fight to defend them on a greater number of fronts, can consider itself *more rational* than the other classes in the sense Norbert Elias gives that adjective. It thereby aspires to take up again the *civilising process* that the other classes have abandoned or betrayed. In any case, it's definitely all about the sequel we add to civilisation.

22. Taking on responsibility, on every issue, on every territory, for the world we live in by explicitly connecting it to the world we live off, *extends the horizon* for action. It's this extension of the horizon that entitles the ecological class to see itself as being *more legitimate* when it comes to defining the *sense of history*. The other classes, hemmed in by the sole horizon of production and the nation states, remain in constant denial of the importance of engendering practices. To further pursue the parallel suggested by Elias, just as the bourgeois class, during its ascent, blasted the aristocracy for its overly narrow vision of its values, similarly the new ecological class contests the legitimacy of the old ruling classes, paralysed by the crisis, and incapable of finding a credible way out of the venture of modern politics and history. It's from this that the new class can draw its energy, its potential power to bring people together, and, not to mince words, *its pride*.

23. In taking up the definition of what's rational so as to change the course of history, the ecological class contests the current ruling classes' role as what Bruno Karsenti calls the *pivotal class*, the one around which the distribution of political positions is organised. Political ecology then emerges from its infancy, stops being an adventitious movement and, above all, stops getting its bearings by reference to the old social classes, stuck as they were in the relations of production alone. It finds itself having the right to criticise what were till now the 'ruling' classes because they weren't able to see the limits of production by restricting economisation, or gear up for the shift to engendering practices, or find a way out that wasn't simply national. By definition, the ecological class changes the distribution between domestic policy and foreign policy: the outside world comes into the inside world. In classical terms, we could say that the liberal tradition, largely shared by the socialist traditions, *betrayed* its own project of development and progress. In the face of the scale of a catastrophe they weren't able to foresee, those ruling classes no longer have any right whatsoever to claim to act *in the name of any kind of rationality*. For this reason, they no longer have any legitimacy whatsoever when it comes to defining the sense of history or garnering the *respect* of the other classes, which they claimed till now to be dragging along behind them. Hence the derision they excite among other classes. Extending the action horizon outside production and beyond the framework defined by the nation states – this, from now on, is the task of the ecological class that's forming. Through this project it, too, in its turn, can hope to drag the other classes along behind it.

24. This reorientation needs to be made clear as soon as possible, because the betrayal on the part of the ruling classes has generated numerous movements, in response, and they've started claiming an attachment to identity, seeking protection inside more or less narrow borders according to the old model of 'our land and our dead'. Well, that narrow definition of territory is even more removed from the direction we need to take, since the denial of habitability conditions it embodies is even more drastic than the dream of globalisation in which the old ruling classes claimed to accommodate modernisation. The land of the reactionaries is even more abstract and barren than that of the globalisers. It's defined only by identity, by the dead, and not by the countless living beings that give it its substance. So the ecological class needs to fight on at least two fronts, against an illusory globalisation and against a return inside borders, since both those movements are out of touch with issues of habitability. In both cases, it's forced to redefine the nature of territories, of all that surrounds, allows, restricts or controls production. Only by carving up the interior and the exterior differently can the ecological class hope to persuade other sectors of the old classes to form an alliance with it in a bid to find other ways of promoting their interests.

25. The ecological class, at loggerheads with the old pivotal classes, sees itself, then, as having a right to define, in its own words and in its own way, the terms soil, territory, land, nation, people, attachment, tradition, boundary, border, and to decide for itself what is 'progressive' and what isn't. It doesn't accept the accusation of being 'reactionary' simply because it's updated the terms territory and soil, which it has completely *repopulated* with a whole host of living things. It claims, on the contrary, to give another meaning to the axis that defines what advances its projects or what, on the contrary, sets them back. To simplify, everything that allows us to superimpose the world we live in and the world we live off in the same legal, affective, moral, institutional and material whole will be considered *progressive* or, better still, *emancipatory*; everything that weakens, ignores or denies this link of superimposition will be considered *reactionary*. As a result, it's now the whole congregation of modernising classes that looks completely *outdated*.

V

A misalignment of affects

26. Observers have long been amazed that neither certainties nor threats have brought about a mass mobilisation on a par with the scale and degree of the urgency. And yet, alarm bells have been ringing for forty years; for twenty years, they've been drilling into everyone's ears; and for the past decade – particularly over the past year or so – the threat has been burned into the first-hand experience of hundreds of millions of people. So where does the failure to react stem from? It's not enough to cite the disinformation campaigns, the power of the lobby groups, or people's mental inertia. None of that has ever stopped millions of activists from throwing themselves wholeheartedly into their battles; they've always understood perfectly well that mobilising, by definition, means confronting that kind of enemy. What we need to understand is why these fairly predictable clashes are managing to intimidate the vast majority, who are ill at ease, and dazed at feeling incapable of taking action. In this indefinitely protracted 'phoney war', there's something so inconsistent with our usual capacities to respond to an obvious threat that we need to keep trying to work out what equipment would be needed finally to translate certainty, anxiety, guilt or befuddlement into general mobilisation.

27. Last century, the mobilising values par excellence were prosperity, liberation, liberty. As soon as those flags were waved, those targets singled out, the most spineless of citizens took themselves for true warriors. It was those powerful affects that launched the old classes into developing production and holding out promises of wealth and freedom. How can they be expected to go into raptures when they're suddenly told those values of prosperity, liberation and liberty need to be entirely overhauled? As long as such emotions aren't redirected, ecology will always be stopped in its progress by accusations of being boring, limited, of going into reverse. How can ecology sound the death knell and try to get the hordes moving 'forwards', true to the old 'progressive' traditions, when what it calls into question is progress itself? It would never be able to shake off the 'punitive ecology' label. Heading towards maintaining habitability conditions is not yet associated with anything remotely exciting enough. Where's the guarantee of prosperity? Where's the promise of ongoing liberation? How can we maintain the ideal of freedom? How can we suddenly go from promises of 'development' to the still hazy promises of 'envelopment'? It's enough to dampen any vague desire for mobilisation.

28. This explains the importance of defining differently the affects associated with freedom which haven't ceased changing over the course of history. Both the *negative* conceptions of freedom – as that which allows the individual to escape constraints and the grip of the people in power – and the *positive* conceptions of freedom – as that which allows communities to live together autonomously – depend on a prior *delimitation* of individuals or human communities that no longer makes any sense when the world we live off demands to be included in the world we live in. Being free changes meaning when it's a question of getting used to finally *depending* on what supports our existence! Ecology again raises the issue of place and the conception of *limits*: on the one hand, it's at variance with the modern passion for continually overrunning barriers, since it needs to try and 'stay within the limits' of the envelope of the Earth system; on the other, it's discovering, through the sciences of this same Earth system, just how little we know about the latter's limits and how these can be *trespassed upon*. On all subjects and at all scales, those of the nation states as well as of human groups or living organisms, ecology directs its inventory and recovery effort at the limits of the old notions of a limit. By 'emancipation', then, we mean liberation from the narrow register of ideas of liberty explored by liberals and socialists alike, within the sole framework of production at the service of human beings.

29. The same goes for the, apparently contradictory, notions of belonging, identity, attachment, locality, solidarity, community life, the common – notions often associated, due to the prior class history, with the soil, the people, the nation. But the soil the old Moderns have landed on doesn't have a hint of the same properties, the same components, the same 'nature', the same 'identity' as the soil the old-style progressives claimed to have left behind. So there's nothing to stop us from *reinvesting* these ideas with a positive new meaning. There is in this new apprenticeship in dependence an opportunity to redefine freedom and the quest for autonomy. The more dependent we are, the better. How contrary to our habits it is, though, this quest for the 'ties that liberate'!

30. The ecological class is adopting, and claims to have inherited, the values of freedom and emancipation, but it needs to invest these with a sense that's finally compatible with its actual conditions, which the notions of production and a more or less fair distribution of wealth cast aside. If it's true, as Karl Polanyi suggested, that land, labour and money are inalienable and *inappropriable*, this means that, by favouring maintenance of habitability, the ecological class is at last meeting up again with its *true owners*. Descartes didn't see that one coming! Humans don't have ownership of a world, a world has ownership of humans. Humans are the ones who, through construction, are 'masters and possessors of nature'... Living things are the ones who, by definition, *possess themselves*, since they've *made themselves by themselves* and since they've gradually engendered planet Earth – or at least the minuscule part of it that's habitable – through a process rightly known as *sui generis*, having engendered itself by itself.

31. This means nature isn't a victim to be protected; it's what possesses us. That's the sense of the proud slogan of the activists known as the *zadistes*: 'We are nature defending itself'... We don't need to repent in the face of poor victims; we need to withstand a hard-nosed new takeover by our true owners... An army of legal experts is in the process of drawing conclusions about what this turnaround means, even for legislation. Engendering practices that allow us to maintain, amplify and repair the habitability of living conditions have once again become the right thing to seek out and look after. What we're living through is the exact opposite of the famous *enclosures* episode. Suddenly, it's humans that find themselves well and truly enveloped, turned and *enclosed* – not to say confined! But the trick is to work out how to make such a subversion of values *positive*. How can we turn the following expression *into common sense*: 'I am dependent, that's what frees me, I can finally act'? How can we make this the new matrix of an expanded conception of solidarity and emancipation?

32. We can see why, for the moment, the long-awaited mobilisation is both inevitable and endlessly delayed. The affects are not *aligned* to the point of creating unthinking habits. And the terrible thing is that we don't have time to set these up one by one and in the right order. It took several centuries for the liberals and then the socialists to invent conditioned reflexes that have become the wheels of various mobilisations in favour of development. Without such a renewal of the components of a common culture, an enormous lag has been created between the values associated with the old social classes and those that need to be promoted by the ecological class. By not getting involved enough in these battles, the ecological class hasn't liberated the political culture from its overly narrow gamut of feelings, arts, works, themes, images, narratives. As a result, it sorely lacks an *aesthetic* capable of fuelling the *political passions* roused by the classes it's fighting. The Great Derangement Amitav Ghosh talks about doesn't yet seem to have *deranged* it enough! For the moment, political ecology has pulled off the feat of either panicking hearts and minds or making people yawn with boredom... Hence the paralysis it too often induces when it comes to action.

VI

A different sense of history in a different cosmos

33. If we continue to explore the sources of this powerlessness to act collectively, what we find, on top of the misalignment of affects, are two elements that largely explain the troubling attitudes of guilty resignation, anxious inertia, wishful thinking – all these *sad passions* so characteristic of the times. It's as if we were hesitating about the sense of the history that's supposedly sweeping us along. And, to complicate the whole thing further, we're not sure about nature, or, to put it more clearly, about the substance of the world we're supposed to take action in. It's become *alien* to us. In the literal sense, 'we're no longer at home'. In spite of all the movements and counter-movements of previous eras, you could say that people then 'knew where they were going', since they were *modernising* themselves. And, on top of that, they could count on something immensely reassuring: a material world that was pretty stable, predictable and familiar. Sharing such certainties meant being able to react rapidly at the first signs of danger.

34. A sense of history doesn't fall out of the sky. As the emergence of other classes shows, it needs to be forged, spread, established, performed. To make an 'English working class', bit by bit, according to E. P. Thompson's description, takes a century. We might recall the lengthy invention of 'modernity' and how much ink was necessary to make its movement 'irreversible' and 'exciting'. Right up until it actually flipped in front of our very eyes! As Elias has amply documented, there's nothing necessary about the advance of a class. No Providence, no Zeitgeist, has ever driven those claiming to define the sense of European history, as is pretty painfully attested by the wilful blindness of the 'bourgeois classes' on climate issues throughout the twentieth century. Ecological culture would be way off the mark to think that 'time is on our side', whatever its followers are doing. It was the very idea of an inevitable 'modernisation front' that perverted all the promises made by the ruling classes over the course of the past century. No more than there is an inevitable modernisation front, we shouldn't expect an irreversible 'ecologisation front'. Again, we shouldn't even count on the scale of the catastrophe under way to change people's minds, contrary to what the following diabolically false phrase once drilled into us: 'Where danger lies, there lies also what saves us.' Nothing will save us, especially not danger. Success will depend entirely on our capacity to seize opportunities as they crop up.

35. If the old ruling classes betrayed us, it was precisely because they believed they brought a sense of inevitable history, an indisputable *telos*, and this made them insensitive to the nature of the *space* in which that history would supposedly unfold. The brutal return of planetary limits prevents the ecological class from repeating the mistake of the other classes, which claimed to be the *avant-garde* of a movement nothing could stop. By claiming to embody the future *in advance*, those so-called 'rational' classes completely ruled out having misgivings about their own future. Without saying so, they were heading for a utopia that rapidly ebbed away. The world to which modernisation blindly led quite simply doesn't exist.

36. The most troubling thing for the ecological class is that it needs to dispute the very idea of a sense, of *a single sense*, of history. The obligation to splice together the world we live off and the world we live in forces us to think of the sense of history not as a movement forward, the way the Moderns thought of it, as they merrily cut the past off from the future behind them, but as a multiplication of ways of *inhabiting* and *taking care* of engendering practices, in total indifference to what belongs to the past, the present or the future. History is thereby no longer seen as a rallying on a coherent front delineating the famous and one and only 'arrow of time', but as a *scattering* in all directions that recaptures and repairs what the old sense of history sought to oversimplify.

37. So, the kind of *subversion* appropriate to this class is as far removed as possible from the 'revolutionary' spirit of the past, with its famous 'convergence of struggles', even as it's still a matter of a break, and one much more radical and much more revolutionary than those that aimed at taking over the means of production alone. This is where we can see the point of the multiplicity, diversity and particularity of the countless struggles activists are engaged in, on all issues and at all scales. How can we give a single sense to a history that, quite the reverse, yields every time to the lesson of living things which, for their part, each have their own way of *making their own history*, just as we make ours?

38. The unity of action of earlier times – at least, as we imagine them in retrospect – was made possible by the fact that, for the modernised, there was only a single material world known to Science. Well, the source of our current trouble is that we're no longer called on to react in that same world. To put it as anthropologists would, we've switched *cosmology*. The harsh experience of the present pandemic allows us to realise this more clearly. The befuddlement of an entire civilisation, forced to adjust to the presence of the virus, announces, under-scores and reinforces this civilisation's inability to react rapidly enough to the New Climate Regime. In the face of this New Regime, we're as helpless as the old 'primitives' startled by the modernisation that devastated their world. From now on, the ill-adapted, under-developed 'primitives', incapable of reacting to the shock of this 'demodernisation', are us!

39. Moderns in the age of development felt *at ease* in nature. Their cosmological model, if we care to take a canonical example, would have been Galileo's inclined plane, which allowed them to calculate the law of falling bodies. Everything had to be like this model. What do you do when the model, the canonical example, is a virus that never stops spreading from mouth to mouth, never stops infecting, mutating, surprising us, and which the sciences, henceforth in the plural, far from mastering, have to track by evolving like it does? For people who counted on the reactions of the old world, the disarray is total: we're no longer humans in nature, but living beings among other living beings freely evolving with and against us and which all take part in the same *terra forming*. In a Galilean world, the epidemic would be a crisis on the way to being resolved; in the world we live in, Covid won't stop forcing us to mutate like it does. That's a terrible lesson to have to learn.

40. This is the root cause of our inability to react: it's as if you were quietly getting ready to build a brick wall and were suddenly asked to contain an epidemic. Everything's shifting, everything's evolving, everything's mutating. To the point where you start having doubts about the world's resistance or even *its substance*. There used to be a framework that didn't react to our actions; now it does react, and at all levels – virus, climate, humus, forest, insects, microbes, oceans and rivers. Suddenly, intimidated, lost, clumsy, we literally no longer know how to *conduct ourselves*. A bit like those hapless souls now required 'to finally get themselves onto the Internet'. We no longer know how to 'get ourselves onto' anything whatever, and especially not how to 'get ourselves *into* the world'. Engendering issues are beyond us. Strangers in our own land, we're disoriented, strongly tempted to throw in the towel – when everything ought to be driving us to act, and fast. It's this cosmological shift that's probably the source of these sad passions that the ecological class needs to diagnose and for which it needs swiftly to invent therapies, if it wants to have a chance one day of wielding power.

VII

The ecological class is potentially in the majority

41. Drawing up a list of the pathologies that need to be treated isn't a demonstration of cruelty but quite the opposite: it's an act of elementary realism. As long as the great masses haven't turned to action to get themselves out of the traps of production, we'll have to continue to probe the underlying cause of their inertia. Fortunately, the picture is quite different if, instead of concerning ourselves with people vaguely ashamed of their torpor, we turn to those who have, long ago, got ready for battle. With these particular people we're finally going to be able to 'be counted'. That's the whole paradox of this 'phoney war': on the one hand, the cause of ecology seems marginal; on the other, everyone has already, in fact, switched paradigms.

42. The ecological class takes over from all the past battles, which revealed, every time, new actors till then considered negligible. In actual fact, the participants whose engendering practices are indispensable to production have only *multiplied* over the course of history. So they are natural allies. First and foremost, obviously, that was the role played by the proletariat in the production of wealth, in the sense of the socialist traditions. Next, it was the role the feminist movements brought to light by showing the connection between the invention of the economy and the longstanding oppression of women. It's also what postcolonial movements never stop pointing to by demonstrating the importance of colonisation and unfair trading in the accumulation of wealth. The multifaceted revelation of the role and of the limits of living beings and the Earth system consequently *needs to be added to* this long series, since it shows how incredibly *limited* the enclosure of production was, and still is. We might take this sentence of David Graeber's: 'Nowadays, if one speaks of "wealth producers", people will automatically assume one is referring not to workers but to capitalists', and rephrase it: 'Nowadays, if one speaks of "wealth producers", people will auto-matically assume one is referring not to living beings but to capitalists.' As we can see, the number of potential members of (ecological) peoples is already vast – provided we underline the continuity between the different movements that have made them visible.

43. The point of kicking the habit of think-ing about relations of production alone is also that you can then reweave a link with what we call *indigenous peoples* – a quarter of a billion of Earth's inhabitants, all the same! – who've managed to resist the grip of 'development'. An alliance that's all the more important because these people have been struggling *from inside* the limits of nation states to subvert those states' land grabs, and because they're changing the temporal direction of progress, without resort-ing to the old arrow of history. And they're doing so even as they multiply innovations to do with what the existence of a *people inhabiting* a land might actually mean. Far from representing the past of productive development, they instead point to the completely contemporary uses of engendering practices we're going to have to invent. The lesson is a bitter one, but it's the old 'primitives' that now have to teach the new ones how to resist modernisation!

44. Another crucial asset for defining this new class is to be sought in the stunning reversal of engendering ties that the New Climate Regime sets up *between the generations*. Disconnecting the world we live in from the world we live off is not, in fact, a simple question of space, but also of time. Living off the future has the consequence of dumping on the next generations the task of fixing the problems of the present – only, later! Hence the impression of having been betrayed by our elders and of finding ourselves, in the literal sense, *without a future*. The future has been used up in advance. Whereas, in the globalisation period, 'the youth cult' served as a signpost for heading towards the future, the sudden revolt of young people who feel betrayed instead consists of seeing the old, and more specifically the *baby boomers* (the old 'young'!), as spoilt, immature teenagers. Youth no longer represents, as it once did, the future of the system of production that turns the archaism of the oldies on its head, but the reverse – the *oldness* of engendering issues that the older generations have deliberately sacrificed. Plenty of forces to recruit there!

45. Large swathes of the intellectual classes already back this extension of the horizon that potentially gives the new ecological class its own form of rationality, so contrary to the 'rationalist' pretensions of the old ruling classes. This is clearly the case with the scientists engaged in one capacity or other in the new Earth system sciences and who've already weathered the great battles imposed by the climate deniers. It's also the case with engineers and inventors, whose desire for innovation has been shattered by the narrow constraints of production. All the intellectual and scientific professionals are ready to pit their rationality against the economy of knowledge and 'rational evaluation' of their work. Innovators have been dispossessed of their inventiveness, but academics, too, have been dispossessed of all that allowed them to pursue their research. Between research, engineering and engendering practices, there are, however, hundreds of ties that have been broken but which numerous 'proof workers' would be ready to re-tie. To this ever-growing list we should add all the activists, militants, people of good will, ordinary citizens, peasants, gardeners, industrialists, investors, explorers in one capacity or other, not to mention all those who've seen their territory disappear before their very eyes. All these people might well feel they're part of this class that's forming, even if, for the moment, they're having trouble seeing their ideals in it. If they felt caught up in the same civilising movement, that would end up being a lot of people!

46. Let's not forget to count the religions in this census. They represent huge forces and deep emotions that have already managed, over the course of the centuries, to transform souls, landscapes, the law, the arts. The specific case of Christians is interesting. They were once urged to leave this Earth behind, but now, they sense in ecology a call that could reset their dogmas. Whenever they associate 'ecology' with 'paganism' or 'immanence', Christians stop being allies. But as soon as they see how ecology liberates them from their 'political theology', then their help becomes precious. With their aid we could start to disentangle that modern political theology, which has nothing secular about it, despite its claims, but mashes up cosmologies, theologies and forms of humanism that we really need to learn to unravel, thread by thread. So let's add to our list all those who work, rite after rite, to make sure that the 'cry of the Earth and the Poor' – to take up the beautiful expression (or, rather, cry!) of Pope Francis – is finally heard.

47. If we stand back and assess the situation, we realise there's nothing marginal about the emerging ecological class at all. To rework a famous quote: 'A spectre is haunting Europe and the rest of the world – the spectre of ecologism!' The only thing it's failed to do is *to define itself as the majority*. It's already something like a new third estate: a nothing that aspires to be everything. As with the old third, all it's lacking is the pride of being sure of itself and of its future – as well as some favourable and completely contingent circumstances that would allow it to come to power... For the moment, it's trying to buck itself up by declaring: 'We are the world, we are the future', and even, in a burst of daring: 'We are taking up the civilising process the others have relinquished.' But behind it, we have to admit, there are still not large enough hordes who see themselves in its proud slogans.

48. The emergence of an ecological class organising class struggles and politics around itself and on its own terms seems, for the moment, limited by the extraordinary *scattering* of forces and experiences. To parody another famous quote: 'Political ecology – how many *divisions*?' But that scattering is *welcome* if it's a matter of escaping by all possible means the seemingly ineluctable fate of expanding production. If we always need to be suspicious of upscaling, this is also true in politics. We have to resist the temptation to *come together* in the spirit of the traditional forms of the political offering, which always claims it will knock over any obstacle in its path, through a sudden almighty battering, and move on to better days. In a virus regime, there are no better days. That's not the way time flows for living things. Here again, the need for us to compose, to build, demands that political ecology *slow down* to be able to discern, in its own way, the alliances it needs to forge. In this sense, political ecology, fuelled by this new culture of living beings, must cherish its multiplicity. That's the thing that allows it to explore alternatives in all directions.

VIII

The indispensable and too often abandoned battle of ideas

49. In 1789, the Third Estate had one advantage that the ecological class sorely lacks. By the time it became the Nation, the battle of ideas, in all circles, in all classes, had been 'softening up hearts and minds', as they say, *for a hundred years already*, and had crept into the innermost reaches of the elites. But who's been softening up the elites over the past hundred years for the mutation under way? There has of course been an immense amount of reflective analysis pursued by countless researchers, thinkers, activists, moralists, militants and poets, but that work has not been taken up by the parties known as 'green' and has only barely registered with the ruling classes. Where are those centres of thought in which for decades and every inch of the way, people led the ideological struggle on all the issues flagged above? You get the horrible impression the struggle has barely begun. The other classes have been kicking up a hell of a racket, saturating the media space, filling magazines, TV programmes, the weeklies, monopolising the training of state agents, multiplying management schools and economics departments. But where are the organs of the ecological class? Nothing allows us to fight back at the right scale to achieve *hegemony* in the battle of ideas.

50. And yet, as the history of social movements shows, there's absolutely no reason to assume that the birth of a class able to contest the role of leader against the other classes, disoriented by the cosmological shift, could occur without such ideological work. And so, *without going through* the immense work of establishing a cultural inventory – a task the other classes have had to perform in the past in order to occupy the centre of the public stage. It may be hackneyed, but the Gramscian theme of a 'quest for hegemony' – this 'war of position' that has to be organised well before conducting any 'war of attack' – applies to the emerging class the same as to all the others. So-called 'objective' '*interests*' have never been enough on their own to give rise to a class that's both aware of itself as such and capable of convincing the others to form an alliance with it. If economic interests alone have never sufficed to get your bearings in class struggles, the same goes for 'ecological interests' alone. Every time, it's *the whole culture* that we need to force ourselves to shake up. If it's reluctant to conduct such battles, the ecological class will always remain the rump of a party.

51. Except that it's a lot harder for this class than for the preceding ones. A whole population has to be made sensitive to a switch in cosmology that implies a prodigious *increase* in issues of concern that need to be taken into account. Even if the traditional social classes all understood, implicitly, their *geo*-social dimension, if only by ignoring it, it's this dimension that again becomes primordial. That's because the battles are now all about the occupation, nature, usage and maintenance of territories and subsistence conditions, and this at all scales and over all continents. So, there's a formidable intensification going on here in the battle of ideas, about *what the world is made of*. And that's why, in the end, it's a question of metaphysics. All the details are starting to count. As Baptiste Morizot says, every pack of wolves merits its own philosophy.

52. The switch in cosmology ought to drive the ecological class to seize upon the *humanities* afresh and, using all kinds of media and all kinds of formats, to work out how this new Earth can be expressed and experienced. Social and cultural history show that culture and the *arts* are particularly pertinent, their importance having been recognised and promoted in all previous eras. On this score, then, the ecological class should replicate the evolution of the classes that preceded it, the liberalisms every bit as much as the socialisms, in their claim to define the whole gamut of subjects mobilised by the culture. Poetry, film, novels, music, architecture – nothing should be outside its remit. If you compare the importance of the arts in the invention of liberalism, or the way the left monopolises cultural criticism, you'll notice how lacking official ecology is in these resources. For the moment, the ecological parties are remarkably absent from the arts scene, or, at the very least, don't have anything like the artistic and intellectual clout the old parties enjoyed. Basically it's as if they felt that, since they were concerned with nature, they could forget about culture.

53. This shift in cosmology presupposes a very different use of the sciences from the modern format. All the contentious issues to do with the Earth system go through the mediation of the 'natural' sciences, since these are largely the origin of the ecological class's very consciousness. Without the sciences, what would we know for certain about the destruction of the world? But this doesn't mean that the sciences have taken up the masterful and reassuring role they were able to play in the liberal or socialist epochs, when they allowed people to *dispense with* politics just because 'they knew what to do'. Instead, the new sciences of an Earth fashioned by living things are part and parcel of exploring the always controversial and surprising conditions of the planet's behaviour. In this sense, the sciences are as unstable and agitated as the system whose turbulence they've started to monitor. Scientists *add* their essential role as mouthpieces for the things they're experimenting on to the many mouthpieces taking part in the controversies. So, access to these sciences and the alliances that need to be forged with researchers thereby offer major advantages in the new battle of ideas. But, once again, we're dealing with a vast *expansion* in the number of subjects that need to be taken into account. The battle *for* ideas goes on even in the fabrication of facts. We need to go into the sciences in detail, and carefully check how these facts have been more or less successfully *cooked up*. Yet another culture to develop, but this time a culture of the scientific humanities.

54. The meticulous reworking of all of modern history because of the mutation in cosmology is all the more important as the current demands carried by this movement are constantly stifled by the use of notions inherited from the preceding period, in particular the notions 'nature' and 'protection of nature'. The 'nature' of the Moderns was what production left 'outside' its horizon, all the while incorporating it in the form of a resource. So, it always remained *external* to social concerns, and you had to agree *to get beyond* the interests of society to be able to worry about its fate. By defining itself as a taking up of the ties between the world we live off and the world we live in, the ecological class is freeing actors both from the *radical exteriority* of nature and, at the same time, from its *limitation* to the sole role of resource. But, to make this transformation clear, to get beyond generalities, requires an enormous amount of preliminary work and, so, of research infrastructure that's in working order and well endowed. As well-oiled as the cart may be, it's better to put it *after* the horse – even if the horse drags its hoofs as it plods heavily along.

55. The apparently philosophical disputes over the metaphysics of the Earth and living things can't be set aside just because they're 'too intellectual' or would force us to 'split hairs'. Our predecessors split every one of the concepts necessary to their seizure of the state as finely as they could! Think of the amount of work needed to invent, provide for, look after and maintain that strange monster, the 'selfish and calculating individual', or the 'citizen of a representative government'! Who can fathom the two centuries needed for the invention of 'the social question', of 'society', 'the proletariat' or 'labour value'? And yet there are those who hope to focus the attention of billions of people on the habitability conditions of the planet with no groundwork, no tools, no practice. As if the obvious importance of living beings were going to be enough on its own to convert people by giving them the indispensable capacity for exercising good judgment so as to wage these disarmingly complex diplomatic battles! The risk is that people will be swamped by a deluge of warm and fuzzy feelings without managing to get a single political lever out of it all.

56. And yet, if there's one subject where the shift in sensibility is evident and has become almost universal, it's in the understanding of living things, and the new grasp of the biological. On this score, we're clearly in the process of changing aesthetics. The whole point of class struggles, in Elias's sense of the term, is that they start out with changes in *manners* – likes and dislikes – well before crystallising into conflicts of interest. Ten years ago, the biological was still confused with 'biology', a province of nature known to Science. You had to escape from this province at any cost if you wanted to devote yourself to values, to the symbolic, the human, the spiritual, etc. Today there isn't a book, a magazine, a festival that doesn't talk about 'living things'. But they aren't the same living things as not so long ago. People want to connect with them, to worm their way into their twists and turns, learn from them what the world is woven out of. The same gut bacteria that used to be frowned upon are now welcomed with something like lust! It's from all living things that people now want to relearn values, the symbolic, the human, the spiritual, which were once dismissively positioned *at a remove from* 'biology'. That's a change of tone, style, attitude, a change of sensibility, that Donna Haraway attempted long ago and that many other writers have extended since. Now living things go well beyond the tiny province of biology alone. Which is the most encouraging symptom of the shift in worlds, one that will allow the ecological class to move on from simple disputes over, say, eating meat, to real class conflicts.

IX

Winning power,
but what kind?

57. As the whole history of social movements shows, it takes a very long time to get
manners, values and cultures to align, even
approximately, with the logic of interests; after
that, to spot friends and enemies; then, to
develop that famous 'class consciousness'; and,
lastly, to invent a political platform that allows
classes to express their conflicts in an institutional form. The battle of ideas, then, necessarily precedes the electoral process by a long shot.
It's deluded to think you can throw yourself into
elections while neglecting the huge amount of
groundwork that alone allows you to distinguish
potential allies and antagonists. For want of such
work, electoral successes, even if they're useful
in terms of apprenticeship and propaganda,

can never go far. In any case, what's the good of getting into government without the backing of classes *primed and motivated enough* to *accept the sacrifices* that the new power, at loggerheads with the production regime, will have to impose on them?

58. It might seem incongruous to ask activists who've dropped out of the system, cut ties with the government and avoided appealing to institutions, to suddenly get ready for battle so as to gain a Gramscian hegemony! All those who continue to march to the beat of the production drum have told them they were 'marginalising themselves', and plenty of those thus accused have themselves actually laid claim to being 'marginals'. But along the way something strange has happened: the struggles that looked to be situated in the margins have all become *central* to the survival of all. This is an astonishing reversal, one that turns every erstwhile marginal into a vector of a battle they're going to have to fight, only *big time* and with heaps of people. There is a problem of orientation here, coupled with a change in affects. How can we ensure that the margins – the old periphery, the world we live off – become the centre of everyone's attention, and how can we recast the feelings associated with *marginality* by linking them to the quest for power?

59. The deployment of the ecological class suffers from a problem unusual in social history: it turns on two fronts that are totally opposed. On the one hand, it has to try to seize power from the classes who occupy the government today but have failed; on the other, it has to try to completely change the organisation of government itself. Of course, every class plans to dismantle the administrative organisation of the preceding class, which it finds too hostile to its interests. But, until now, it was always, at the end of the day, about divvying up differently, about amplifying and reorganising the productive forces or, more rarely, redistributing the goods produced more fairly. The Leninists may well have hoped for the 'withering away of the state', but, at the same time, they counted on the inevitable growth of the forces of production; there was no real tension there. How can we envision the organisation of a government that would be *against* production, and so would turn round and head back to its old margins?

60. The old ruling classes could point to a single horizon – one that was always pushed back. As soon as we claim to join together the world we live in and the one we live off, we have to define *two* horizons, in conflict with each other. It would help to have at least an *image* of this battle on two fronts. Let's imagine a circle with a finely drawn edge. At first, the thickness of the edge doesn't seem to matter, it's taken for granted, as an outline. Everyone's attention is directed towards the centre, towards unlimited production. Then, gradually, the edge gets so thin it's threatened with disappearing. As a result, 'marginals' turn round and go back to the edge, followed shortly after by larger and larger masses of people. What was once a resource and demanded to be *extracted* becomes an object of the greatest care, to the point where it's the edge that becomes the *centre* of everyone's attention. The old edge gets thicker and thicker, becomes entangled, piles up, repopulates, to the point where it starts to threaten, to stifle, to strangle the centre, the old centre, the one that threatened to stifle it! There you have the two horizons, the two senses of history, each threatening the other. Either you insist on continuing on towards the old centre, but the edge will oppose that; or you do all you can to enlarge and complicate the edge, but the centre will oppose that.

61. What further complicates the quest for power is that, as soon as the ecological class tries to match up the world we live off and the world we live in so they coincide, it reopens, for each topic, issues of geopolitics, trade and international law, as well as of borders and the type of land use appropriate to nation states. It's a known fact that the current state was designed to allow the dominant classes to exercise their monopoly and to give them access first to modernisation, then to globalisation. The state is in no way designed for the needs of the new ecological class. This mismatch is obvious in the training of its personnel, in the political platform that allows it to define the task of government, as well as in its territorial footprint. What's more, the new relationship demanded by taking the world we live off into account *within the logic* of the world we live in *does not tally with* the distinction and the connection between inside and outside that traditionally defines the *monopoly* of power in nation states (police, taxes, army) or the sense of the word 'sovereign'. On the contrary, the nation state *allows* the radical break between the two worlds that is precisely what we need to mitigate. Since the role of the state is different for the ecological class, so too is the definition of the monopoly it represents, as well as the new distribution between 'foreign' policy and 'national' policy that it is trying to bring about.

62. The division of nation states into checks and mosaic patterns having organised a form of planet grab brutally opposed to any attempt to reconnect the two worlds, the ecological class needs to tackle the controversies over the *planetary* itself, and, with them, the function of states. All the more so as the disintegration of the 'international order', based on development and globalisation, is accelerating before our very eyes, without our being able to imagine any redefinition of old 'supranational' or 'intergovernmental' relations. Marginalised as it is for the moment by the political offering, it's over these issues of recasting the international order and redistributing 'land grabs' that the ecological class would be justified in defining the *sense* or, better still, the *senses* of history. And yet, much like the liberalisms and socialisms, only in a completely different way, it does indeed reopen the question of *universality* and explore the question of how to make multiple forms of power *interdependent*. But since it's based, by definition, on the *superposition* of mutually overlapping territories, and since it's caught between two directions that can each stifle the other, it can't respect any of the classic barriers imposed by the check patterns it's inherited from modern states. More than a chessboard, the space it's now taken upon itself to represent resembles a coat every bit as patchy as Harlequin's.

63. Even if the form this monopoly of power takes is different from the political tradition, the ecological class, too, still needs to orient itself towards *achieving* a monopoly that has to be reinvented. If it fails to do this it will just have to resign itself to powerlessness. As far as it's concerned, all topics are part and parcel of *geopolitics* and every topic necessitates a redrawing of land grabs by states. Hence its own specific difficulty in seeking power. And in doing so while altering its perimeter so that the state apparatus it hopes to occupy defines its functions and its mode of action differently, along with the shape of the territories over which it will exercise its power. In other words, the ecological class can't aspire to define politics by clinging to its marginality or by claiming to be indifferent to the institutions and the workings of current states. It has to occupy the state apparatus on all levels and in all its functions.

64. Not only have the relations between outside and inside been upended, but use of the classic metric that allows us to move from the local to the global has lost all meaning. That cartographic model arose in tandem with production and was developed for its purposes. The redoubtable upscaling was imposed by the needs of production, which structures all relations, through the inevitable question: '*Is it scalable?*' But engendering practices move in a different direction and demand as many measuring instruments as there are situations. The battle against what Anna Tsing calls 'scalability' thereby becomes central. Ecology is neither local nor global – it exists at all scales, and its metrics vary according to each object of study and each subject of dispute. It can't go on being paralysed by localism, or, conversely, by the sudden obligation to 'broaden in scope' in the spirit of the old ways of thinking about society or nature 'as a whole'. It has to develop its own ways of *putting together* collectives and forming 'totalities'. A lesson the virus reminds us of every day!

65. Happily, there is Europe. Despite all the flaws in its bureaucracy, there is in that vast 'thing', if not a source of hope, then at least some kind of experimentation on all the new geopolitical conflicts the ecological class is involved in. It's a massive advantage to be able to count on a power that has successively tried the supra- then the international, but that isn't the national, either. A hesitant power, which doesn't even have a *place* – unless you count an administrative centre in Brussels as the capital of an empire! United Europe is actually delightfully disunited enough, but already completely removed from an old-fashioned state, to redistribute, morsel by morsel, the ingredients that the new forms of power are going to have to assemble some other way. Agriculture, water, pollutants, lobbyists, roads, trains – everything goes through it but, every time, issues, diced into a thousand pieces, are negotiated, discussed, merged, buried in such a fashion that no one state can declare them *its own*. As a result, there's no affair that's really foreign any more and none that's really national. United Europe is an exemplar of a truly life-size experiment in which the redistribution of the inside and outside of states primes the ecological class for its future pivotal role as a class capable of dragging the other classes along behind it. People sometimes lump ecology with United Europe in the same scorn, but that's precisely because both are *more rational* than those that claim to be doing better than them. We just need to see that this superior rationality is revindicated with pride.

X

Filling the emptiness of the public space from below

66. Alas, the ecological class is striving to become self-aware at the very moment when political life is at its most sinister. Not only because of the disintegration of the old parties, not only because of the ongoing evisceration of the state, but because *politics* itself, that complex mix of attitudes, habits, affects, analyses, that curious manner, acquired over the years, of mingling, of using each other, of taking each other on, is disappearing. The very moment we need a massive input of political energy, it's lacking because it hasn't been cultivated. Unless the two phenomena are linked: what has evacuated politics is the fact that, for thirty years now, the New Climate Regime has been weighing more and more heavily on all analyses of interests, on all class relations, on all emotions, but nothing has been done to absorb the formidable effects of this. Hence the appalling emptiness of the public space. The ecological class aims to fill that void.

67. But it can only do so provided it tackles it *from below*, meaning through a *description* of the material world inhabitants find themselves in, having been driven out of their old cosmology into a different one that they still haven't learned to explore. It's in this sense that the ecological class is taking up the *materialist* tradition again. Let's go through the whole sequence again backwards: for you to vote, there need to be *parties*; for there to be parties, you need to have gathered, stylised and stabilised *grievances* into something like programmes; for there to be grievances, each person needs to be able to define their own *interests*, which allow them to draw up fronts of potential allies and adversaries. But how can you have interests if you can't describe in enough detail the concrete situations you find yourself in? If you don't know *what you depend on*, how will you know what you'll need to *defend*? Now, this first phase is lacking because of the speed and especially the scope of the mutation under way. And so, the rest doesn't follow. We need to start by the roots – the *grassroots*.

68. In the absence of any shared, provable, demonstrable sense of having interests, and of the conflicts and entanglements between them, all that's left to participants – no one exactly dares call them 'citizens' any more – is to fall into the saddest passions of all: *complaint* and *recrimination*. The most depressing thing about this is that the complaints are addressed to some mysterious entity supposedly capable of giving the plaintives satisfaction. But, alas, this mythical agent is the old state, designed for the old ruling classes and reduced today to a *shadow*. Some, at the bottom, no longer know how to put their grievances for want of knowing exactly where they find themselves and, so, who their enemies are; others, at the top, are incapable of listening to what's being asked of them and continue to respond with the blunt instruments of the formerly modernising state. It's a case of the dumb talking to the deaf. And naturally the situation gets worse every election cycle, with

the dumb more and more furious that they're
not being heard, and the deaf furious that their
solutions aren't being greeted the way they
should be. Hence the impression that the public
space has become unacceptably violent. We can
blame social media all we like, lament the 'rise
of incivility', but the crisis is much more profound: there has been a state for reconstruction,
a state for modernisation, a state (very much
shaken up) for globalisation, but there is no
state for ecologisation. Not one civil servant, not
one elected representative, can tell us how to go
from *growth* – and its associated miseries – to
prosperity – and its associated sacrifices.

69. The definition of interests, limited till
now by the domination of the economy, can
be freed up by the cosmological shift under
way. Change the definition of the territory, of
its components and commensals, of what ena-
bles engendering practices, and you change the
definition of interests, too, along with the shape
of the land you inhabit. Your territory is *whatever you depend on,* no matter how far you have
to go to feel what holds you in its grip. This is
why an intensive labour of *description* of lived

situations is the indispensable first step towards the emergence of a class that actually sees itself as capable of defining the sense of history. Any description of living conditions is first a *self-description* that reveals the overlap between the world you live in and the world you live off, and so redraws who you are, on what territory you stand, at what period in time, and what horizons you're gearing up to act on.

70. Describing doesn't just mean seeing yourself from the outside, objectively; it also means finding your way and orienting yourself with and in opposition to others undergoing *the same ordeals* of self-description. These shared descriptions thus involve a profound transformation in each person's positions and in the political affects associated with the cosmological mutation. Only when the ties of interdependence with engendering practices have multiplied can we begin to make out the numerous divides between continuing on with production or devoting ourselves to maintaining habitability conditions and the prosperity that results from that. In this sense, exercises in self-description go with the *metamorphosis* in the political situation, which pivots from production towards maintenance of habitability by *extending* the horizon on which history unfolds – and thereby the relative rationality of the actors. The more they describe themselves, the more they give vent to their grievances, the more audible those grievances become to the others. These collective descriptions are a bit like the concrete blocks laid under water to give crustaceans, algae, corals and fish an opportunity to multiply once again. Politics bounces back. The abyss between the dumb and the deaf diminishes accordingly. It can happen very fast.

71. Through another stroke of bad luck, at the very moment we need it most regarding all these issues involving new methods of investigation, the university has been sacked, the research system sacrificed, education scorned. Well, the ecological class needs a research system adapted to this reversal. The university remains the Humboldt model, a caricature of the modernisation movement, with a pointy end, the avant-garde of 'fundamental research', which is supposed to *trickle down* all the way to the common folk – just like profits. But the exigencies of the times are exactly the reverse: given the state of overwhelming ignorance we're all in over what it means to inhabit an Earth that reacts to our actions, we need *even more* research that's *even more* incorruptibly fundamental. But this basic research must *support* all those who need to be assisted in the exploration of their new living conditions. Far from the trickle-down model, what we have to manage to set up is a short-circuit between the most rigorous requirements of fundamental research and the humble situations where that research is *road-tested* so we can define future innovations. Reversing the development schema is as valid for research in the social or natural or hybrid sciences as it is for all the rest. The delicate art of *science policy* isn't commonly discussed among ecologists, yet its importance is decisive.

72. As John Dewey taught us, 'the state is always to be reinvented'. But it always needs a *people*, a *public* that precedes it, teaches it and guides it. It is merely their provisional, and easily corruptible, delegate. This people is what the ecological class must agree to represent if it's to play its role as a new pivotal class. Till now, the other classes were invited to *follow* the ruling classes on the road to modernisation, supposedly either sharing its benefits or gathering up its crumbs. The whole question is whether the interests of those classes can resonate with the interests of the ecological class. To date, the latter hasn't known how to align its struggle against production with the *current* concerns, desires, habits and interests of the other classes. And yet, the support of those classes is indispensable to acceptance of the immense sacrifices we'll have to go through to change regime. If you've found the pandemic hard to live through, imagine a situation where the measures that need to be taken are a hundred times more restrictive on issues we value as much as health. And without an even vaguely legitimate state to propose them – not to mention impose them.

73. Despite appearances, the ecological class seeks to resist the hierarchy imposed by the old ruling classes. For the latter, there was the vanguard and there was the rearguard. The progress brought about by development was assumed to promote an arrangement that would be acceptable to all the classes, called upon as they were to develop in concert and in the same direction. But the new class struggle has disrupted that order. Heading towards *envelopment* demands a very different map from *development*. The ecological class defines the old rearguard very differently: society, to wheel in Polanyi once again, has always *resisted* economisation. And what are known as the 'popular classes' have always been the first to resist, to say nothing of the fact that they're the ones who have to bear the brunt of the destruction system head-on. Very far from being a 'latte-sipping-undergrad' affair, the ecological class is quite simply reconnecting with the ancestral culture of resistance to the non-sense of economisation that tries to annihilate anthropological ties. It recognises in the old rearguard those who are *readier* to try to solve the issues of liveability than the ex-ruling classes, and *much nearer* furthermore to the old margins. It's this shift that makes the ecological class *genuinely* and not merely potentially in the majority. The ecologists aren't drawing the other classes *to them* – quite the opposite: they're joining those classes at last.

74. It's on this last decisive point that the conflicts are playing out: the first, the conflict between the classes, defining 'conflict' the old-fashioned way; and a *second-tier* conflict between the traditional classes and the redistribution of *classifications* performed by political ecology in its quest for allies. People who are totally opposed from the viewpoint of their class membership find themselves close to their 'class enemies' when ecological issues suddenly crop up; and conversely, people who are close turn into bitter enemies. But these switches in affiliation can't occur without the work of politics that allows people to take each other on as they invent procedures, sites, places, opportunities to allow the work of re-description to move on from the conventional view of the social world to a version that's more clearly articulated and more realistic. We don't need much time at all – provided we find an appropriate procedure – to completely transform the cartography of allies and adversaries. The invention of such procedures is what will ultimately determine the success or failure of the redistribution under way to the benefit of the ecological class and its pivotal role.

75. At the moment we can only divine the emergence of this ecological class through a thick fog. That's why it's useful to try to find parallels, either by looking at the history of social and cultural classes, or by drawing on the civilising process and comparing its battles to define politics with the battles of the bourgeoisie in the days when it appeared to express modern purpose. It goes without saying that everything will unfold differently. That's why we need to be ready to seize unforeseen opportunities.

76. In drawing up a list of all the points we'll need to work on together to bring about this famous class consciousness, we could come to the discouraging conclusion that there's so much to change, and on issues so diverse, that the ecological class has no chance of ever competing with the current ruling classes. Especially as it's running out of time. On the other hand, though, everything's probably already in place since, deep down, people know perfectly well that they've switched worlds and that they now inhabit a different Earth. As Paul Veyne noted, the great upheavals are sometimes as simple as the movement a sleeper makes turning over in bed. . .

Will ecology ever be politics as usual?

Postface to the English edition of the Memo

There are times when it's tempting to give in to despair. That's certainly the case for many of us today when we see that people trying to extricate themselves from the tragic imbroglios of the climate mutation now also have to share the traumatic experience of a new European war of conquest and annihilation.

For the authors of the above text, there is an added occasion for pain: never has the idea of an 'ecological class that's self-aware and proud' seemed so remote! Especially in France where, a few months after the book came out, it emerged that in the national elections the Greens didn't even manage to reach the 5 per cent bar that would have allowed them to have their *costs* reimbursed by the state. Pride, you say? More like shame! Shame at not being able to react effectively to the tyranny of a Russian despot, and shame again at not being up to the task of mobilising the right energies to tackle the war on climate being waged by a whole lot of other despots.

What is so terrifying for Europeans is to realise that, in the last few months, they may well have been living through the end of a period that will from now on be known as a new 'interwar' period. Older generations realised to their great dismay, in 1940, that an interwar period had dramatically closed. In the same way, we realise with no less dismay, in 2022, that the period which opened in 1945 is now coming to a close. End of the parenthesis.

The reason why we might not have been utterly mistaken in our tentative quest for an 'ecological class' is that a large chunk of ecological conflicts are now included in the strange war that closes this new parenthesis.

In the same way that Covid, in just a few weeks, fostered a new understanding of the many microbes we live with, and demonstrated how quickly whole nations could react to a new threat, the war on European soil forced a reckoning with the material conditions of European prosperity and showed us, once again, how quickly states and people were ready to cope with a new tragedy.

A few days after the invasion of Ukraine by Putin's tanks, tattooed with the ghoulish Z, it became clear to everybody that financing the dictator to the tune of hundreds of millions of euros by buying his oil and gas gave the war an even more monstrous and farcical face. Something had to be done to wean Europeans as fast as possible off imports of Russian oil and gas. So, suddenly, a move that had started as a *military* decision to maintain autonomy and protect European sovereignty was able to turn into an *ecological* decision to obtain at last a shift away from carbon-based fuel that activists had long been clamouring for without budging European states from out of their complacency. For Ukraine's sake, a major plank of the ecologists' programme had to be realised as urgently as possible, having proved impossible to obtain 'for the planet's sake'. The two types of war, the one on climate, the other on a free European nation, had partially to merge.

To this day we have no proof that anything will really be done quickly enough to deprive Russia of oil money before the war ends, especially when the injunction 'drill, baby, drill' is now heard everywhere in the panic of nations gasping for energy. But what has changed the game more durably is that it is now clear to everyone that there are *two types* of territorial conflict that share many features. The one waged by an empire like Russia to invade, occupy, destroy and annihilate another country, and the other one industrial countries wage on one another and on the rest of the world, through countless decisions on energy, finance, pollution and commerce, to invade, occupy, destroy and annihilate other territories and the forms of life that made them habitable. On top of that, in both types of war the threat of annihilation is being drawn out either by renewed appeals to atomic weapons or by the relentless destruction of the biosphere. Two Armageddons at once, plus a pandemic – that's too hard to swallow.

In our memo we argue that ecologists have the greatest difficulty in tuning the general public to the right range of affects necessary to move away from the obsession with production.

When the war started, we had an illustration that the *first* type of territorial war triggers passions much more mobilising than the *second* type of territorial invasion. States and public opinion sort of knew instantly how to behave collectively to help Ukraine, how to open borders to refugees, to send weapons, to choke the Russian economy through quick decisions – and hopefully we still do. No similar drives, no quick decisions on the part of states, no unanimous assent, no call to accept sacrifices, had been vis ible in the other conflicts, which were marked for years, on the contrary, by a painfully slow, hesitant, interrupted path. One type of conflict mobilises people quickly and intensely; with the other, dithering is the name of the game.

In a way this is good. Ecology shouldn't trigger the same types of passions as trench warfare, since the tasks required to repair and maintain the habitability of a territory are utterly different from those involved in production, occupation and war, in its terrifyingly classical version. But this means it remains crucial to explore, refine, amplify and popularise the passions necessary to fight the two territorial conflicts, enmeshed in one another as they are, without resorting solely to the militaristic ethos. What is the most affective and effective equipment for ecological 'warriors'?

To witness the end of this new interwar period is to finally realise that there is nothing in ecological questions that is *not* about one territory dominating another. Or to put it in other words, ecological stakes are now clearly deepening, complicating, spreading and intensifying the most classical *geopolitical* questions. Although it's now clear that ecological questions are about sovereignty, autonomy, international relations, commerce and military strategy, as well as about taking care of the land and rendering the planet habitable again, there is as yet no widely shared manner of integrating all those contradictory goals in one coherent definition of politics.

It would be so comforting to say that, since ecology is *coterminous* with civilisation, there is no need any longer to distinguish between what is economics, what is social justice, what is defence and war and what is caring for nature.

We could then resort to a much older definition of the polity as symbolised in *The Allegory of Good and Bad Government*, found in Siena.

It's true that, in this most famous fresco, no artificial divide is made between what pertains to commerce, architecture, landscape, art, agriculture or civic life. In the prosperous state of affairs run by the Good Government, all those features are enmeshed together just as they are all destroyed together – land, cities, landscape and social relations – in the ruined estate run by the Bad Government. It's as if Lorenzetti had painted in the dystopian part of his triptych a present view of Mariupol or Sievierodonetsk a picture of the tyrant and his retinue included. If we could only bring back this oldest notion of what a good polity is, we could even get rid of the label 'ecology'!

However, it's impossible to say today that the more the 'ecological class' becomes 'self-aware and proud', the less it needs to *specify* its goals, simply merging with what is the most delicate task of all: making sure the habits of *good* government are being maintained. Alas, as we argue in our memo, every item in the equipment necessary to address these different types of territorial conflict has to be made anew: what is a state, what is a territory, what is the meaning of freedom, what is a subject, what is a citizen, and most importantly, what are the classes that are able draw up these many frontlines all at once? If all these questions should be collectively discussed that's because right up to the present day ecology continues to alter profoundly the very content of what is expected in politics. At the end of this new interwar period, even more than before, 'political ecology' remains the name of a war zone.